MUSIC FOR
HOLY WEEK AND EASTER

MUSIC FOR
HOLY WEEK AND EASTER

MIKE ANDERSON

We hope you enjoy the music in this book. Further copies are available
from your local Kevin Mayhew stockist.

In case of difficulty, or to request a catalogue,
please contact the publisher direct by writing to:

The Sales Department
KEVIN MAYHEW LTD
Buxhall
Stowmarket
Suffolk IP14 3BW

Phone 01449 737978
Fax 01449 737834
E-mail info@kevinmayhewltd.com

First published in Great Britain in 2004 by Kevin Mayhew Ltd.

© Copyright 2004 Kevin Mayhew Ltd.

ISBN 1 84417 189 2
ISMN M 57024 281 8
Catalogue No: 1450302

0 1 2 3 4 5 6 7 8 9

Cover design by Angela Selfe
Music setter: Geoffrey Moore
Proof reader: Linda Ottewell

Printed and bound in Great Britain

Contents

1 Children of Jerusalem

Words and music: Mike Anderson

With energy and enthusiasm ($\quad$ = 135)

(All verses)

Chil-dren of Je - ru - sa - lem wel - come Christ the King!

(1) Wave your ol - ive branch - es and loud 'ho - san-nas' sing!
(2) Lay your cloaks be - fore him and loud 'ho - san-nas' sing!
(3) Shout a - gainst op - pres - sion and loud 'ho - san-nas' sing!
(4) Raise your voice for free - dom and loud 'ho - san-nas' sing!

Save us! Save us! Save us King of kings!

Last time to Coda

Chil-dren of Je - ru - sa - lem sing out! Sing out! Here comes your

2 Let me wash your feet

Maundy Thursday

Words and music: Mike Anderson

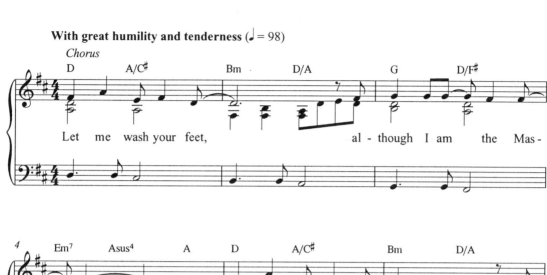

Let me wash your feet, al-though I am the Mas-

-ter. Let me wash your feet, now

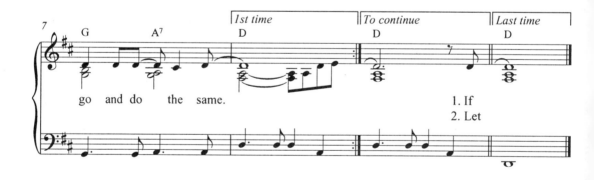

go and do the same.

1. If
2. Let

there is love a - mong you, all will know
faith and hope and love live, with the great-

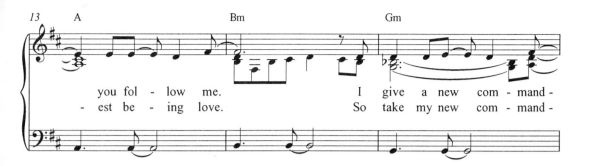

3 Stay, watch and pray

(A Gethsemane Reflection)

Maundy Thursday

Words and music: Mike Anderson

The people repeat 'Stay, watch and pray'
(below) for the entire piece while the Cantor
sings the invocations as Jesus.

A - lone I face this a - gon - y.

Could you not watch with me?

The spi - rit is will - ing, the flesh though is weak!

This cup of suf - fer - ing I'll drink.

The fate - ful hour has come!

Will you be - tray me with a kiss?

Will you de - ny me?

Will you de - ny me?

Will you de - ny me?

Bm7   A2   *Last time rit.*

Stay, watch and pray.

4 This is the wood of the cross

Good Friday

Words and music: Mike Anderson

* *Optional harmony.*

5 The light of Christ

The Easter Liturgy

Words and music: Mike Anderson

With all the joy of the Resurrection! (♩ = 82)

The light of Christ! The light of Christ! The light of Christ! Al - le - lu - ia! The light of Christ! The light of Christ! The light of Christ! Al - le - lu - ia! Al - le - lu - ia! Al - le - lu - ia! Al - le - lu - ia!

* Optional harmony.

6 Rejoice, heavenly powers! The Easter Liturgy

Words and music by Mike Anderson
Based on the Exsultet

2. The price for Adam's sin is paid, (Rejoice! Rejoice!)
   by Jesus' blood we have been saved, (Rejoice! Rejoice!)
   he rose triumphant from the grave! (Rejoice! Rejoice!)
   Rejoice! Rejoice! Rejoice!

3. This night will be as clear as day, (Rejoice! Rejoice!)
   the Morning Star is here to stay, (Rejoice! Rejoice!)
   and he has washed all guilt away! (Rejoice! Rejoice!)
   Rejoice! Rejoice! Rejoice!

4. And now this Easter candle's light, (Rejoice! Rejoice!)
   dispels the darkness of the night, (Rejoice! Rejoice!)
   rejoice in justice, peace and right! (Rejoice! Rejoice!)
   Rejoice! Rejoice! Rejoice!

*If the verses are sung by a solo voice (Celebrant/Cantor), the soloist should
feel free to improvise within the chord structure.*

15

7 I will sing to the Lord
The Easter Liturgy

Words and music by Mike Anderson
Based on Exodus 15

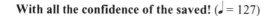

14

Em · · · · B · · · Em

Glo - rious is the Lord who res - cued me!
Phar - aoh's ar - my har - ries me no more!
Your right hand pre - vailed and won the hour!

17

B C D B ⌐3⌐ Em

He is my strength! He is my song, and
En - e - mies fall un - der his pow'r and
Great is your name, end - less your reign, and

20

C Dsus⁴ D D.C.

I will give him praise!
I will give him praise!
I will give you praise!

⊕ CODA

23

G C D G

name! I will praise his name!

26

C D G

I will praise his name!

17

MUSIC FOR
HOLY WEEK AND EASTER

8 Springs of living water flow The Easter Liturgy

Words and music: Mike Anderson

This piece is most effective when used as a round, the parts entering at A, B, C and D.
It can be repeated ad lib. and can vary in intensity.

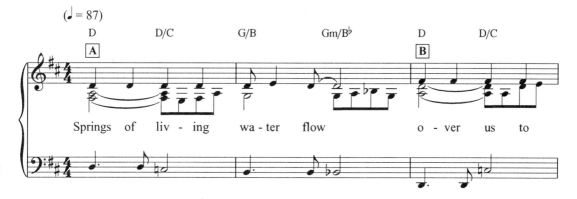

Springs of liv - ing wa - ter flow o - ver us to

make us grow in faith, in hope, in mer - cy and in

love.

9 Think of the love

A Lent to Easter Song

Words and music: Mike Anderson

Verses 1 to 3: poignantly;
Verse 4: triumphantly!

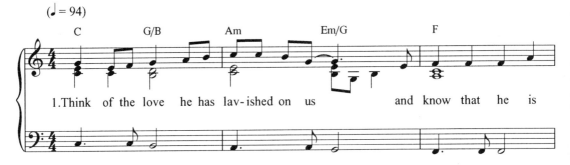

1. Think of the love he has lav-ished on us and know that he is

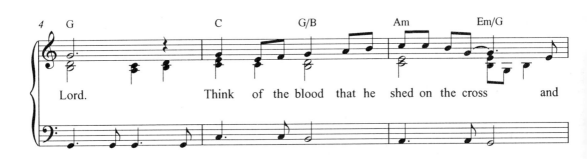

Lord. Think of the blood that he shed on the cross and

know that he is Lord. He bled and

died for us, was glo - ri - fied for us.

Think of the love he has lav-ished on us and know that he is

Lord.

2. Think of the man so reviled and abused — and know that he is Lord.
   Think of his body so broken and bruised and know that he is Lord.
   He bled and died for us — was glorified for us.
   Think of the love he has lavished on us and know that he is Lord.

3. Think of the pain of the nails driven in and know that he is Lord.
   Think of the price that he paid for our sin and know that he is Lord.
   He bled and died for us — was glorified for us.
   Think of the love he has lavished on us and know that he is Lord.

4. Think of the day when he rose like the sun — and know that he is Lord.
   Think of the freedom his victory won — and know that he is Lord.
   He died but now he lives — his Spirit freely gives.
   Think of the love he has lavished on us and know that he is Lord.

During Lent (and especially on Good Friday), sing only verses 1 to 3.
On Easter Day and at all other times, add verse 4.

1 Children of Jerusalem

Palm Sunday

Mike Anderson

With energy and enthusiasm ($\quad$ = 135)

Last time to Coda

2 Let me wash your feet

Maundy Thursday

Mike Anderson

With great humility and tenderness (♩ = 98)

C instrument

1st time

Last time | To continue

Fine

D.C.

3 Stay, watch and pray

(A Gethsemane Reflection)

Maundy Thursday

Mike Anderson

*Repeat ad lib. for the
duration of the song.*

4 This is the wood of the cross

Good Friday

Mike Anderson

With great reverence (♩ = 68)

5 The light of Christ

The Easter Liturgy

Mike Anderson

With all the joy of the Resurrection! (♩ = 82)

6 Rejoice, heavenly powers!

The Easter Liturgy

Mike Anderson

7 I will sing to the Lord

The Easter Liturgy

Mike Anderson

With all the confidence of the saved! ($\quarternote$ = 127)

8 Springs of living water flow

The Easter Liturgy

Mike Anderson

9 Think of the love

A Lent to Easter Song

Mike Anderson

Verses 1 to 3: poignantly; Verse 4: triumphantly!

MUSIC FOR
HOLY WEEK AND EASTER

CONGREGATION

Congregation

1 Children of Jerusalem

Palm Sunday

Words and music: Mike Anderson

2 Let me wash your feet

Maundy Thursday

Words and music: Mike Anderson

With great humility and tenderness (♩ = 98)

Chorus

Let me wash your feet, al-though I am the Mas - ter.

Let me wash your feet, now go and do the same.

1st time

To continue | *Last time*

1. If there is love a - mong you, all will know
2. Let faith and hope and love live, with the great-

you fol - low me. I give a new com - mand -
- est be - ing love. So take my new com - mand -

D.C.

- ment, that you love as I love you!
- ment, go and love as I love you!

3 Stay, watch and pray
(A Gethsemane Reflection)

Maundy Thursday

Words and music: Mike Anderson

(♩ = 100)

Stay, watch and pray.

4 This is the wood of the cross

Good Friday

Words and music: Mike Anderson

With great reverence (♩ = 68)

Cantor/Celebrant

This is the wood of the cross on which hung our Sa-viour!

Congregation

Come and wor-ship! Come and wor-ship! Come and wor-ship the Sa-viour of all.

Sa-viour of all! Sa-viour of all! Sa-viour of all!

Come and wor - ship! Come and wor - ship! Come and wor-ship the Sa-viour of all!

* Optional harmony

5 The light of Christ

The Easter Liturgy

Words and music: Mike Anderson

With all the joy of the Resurrection! (♩ = 82)

The light of Christ! The light of Christ! The light of Christ! Al -le -lu -ia! The

Al -le -lu - ia! Al -le -lu - ia! Al -le -lu - ia!

light of Christ! The light of Christ! The light of Christ! Al - le - lu - ia!

* Optional harmony

6 Rejoice, heavenly powers!

The Easter Liturgy

Words and music by Mike Anderson
Based on the Exsultet

2. The price for Adam's sin is paid, (Rejoice! Rejoice!)
by Jesus' blood we have been saved, (Rejoice! Rejoice!)
he rose triumphant from the grave! (Rejoice! Rejoice!)
Rejoice! Rejoice! Rejoice!

3. This night will be as clear as day, (Rejoice! Rejoice!)
the Morning Star is here to stay, (Rejoice! Rejoice!)
and he has washed all guilt away! (Rejoice! Rejoice!)
Rejoice! Rejoice! Rejoice!

4. And now this Easter candle's light, (Rejoice! Rejoice!)
dispels the darkness of the night, (Rejoice! Rejoice!)
rejoice in justice, peace and right! (Rejoice! Rejoice!)
Rejoice! Rejoice! Rejoice!

7 I will sing to the Lord

The Easter Liturgy

Words and music by Mike Anderson
Based on Exodus 15

With all the confidence of the saved! (♩ = 127)

Chorus

I will sing to the Lord, glo - ri - ous his tri - umph!

I will sing to the Lord, I will praise his name!

Last time to Coda — *To repeat chorus*

To verses

name!
1. He has thrown my foes in - to the sea!
2. I stand safe and sound up - on the shore!
3. Your right hand is glo - ri - ous in pow'r!

Glo - rious is the Lord who res - cued me! He is my strength!
Phar - aoh's ar - my har - ries me no more! En - e - mies fall
Your right hand pre - vailed and won the hour! Great is your name,

D.C.

He is my song, and I will give him praise!
un - der his pow'r and I will give him praise!
end - less your reign, and I will give you praise!

CODA

name! I will praise his name! I will praise his name!

8 Springs of living water flow

Words and music: Mike Anderson

This piece is most effective when used as a round, the parts entering at A, B, C and D.
It can be repeated ad lib. and can vary in intensity.

(♩ = 87)

A | B

Springs of liv - ing wa - ter flow o - ver us to make us grow in

C | D | *Last time*

faith, in hope, in mer - cy and in love.

9 Think of the love

A Lent to Easter Song

Words and music: Mike Anderson

Verses 1 to 3: poignantly;
Verse 4: triumphantly!

1. Think of the love he has lav-ished on us and know that he is Lord. Think of the blood that he shed on the cross and know that he is Lord. He bled and died for us, was glo-ri-fied for us. Think of the love he has lav-ished on us and know that he is Lord.

2. Think of the man so reviled and abused — and know that he is Lord.
   Think of his body so broken and bruised and know that he is Lord.
   He bled and died for us — was glorified for us.
   Think of the love he has lavished on us and know that he is Lord.

3. Think of the pain of the nails driven in and know that he is Lord.
   Think of the price that he paid for our sin and know that he is Lord.
   He bled and died for us — was glorified for us.
   Think of the love he has lavished on us and know that he is Lord.

4. Think of the day when he rose like the sun — and know that he is Lord.
   Think of the freedom his victory won — and know that he is Lord.
   He died but now he lives — his Spirit freely gives.
   Think of the love he has lavished on us and know that he is Lord.

During Lent (and especially on Good Friday), sing only verses 1 to 3.
On Easter Day and at all other times, add verse 4.

Please photocopy this page

KEVIN MAYHEW EASY COPYRIGHT CLEARANCE

The words and music in this book are protected by copyright and may not be reproduced in any way without the proper permission.

A licence to reproduce the congregational part only of *Music for Holy Week and Easter* for non-commercial use may be obtained from the Kevin Mayhew Copyright Department by sending a copy of this page together your payment.

Name of Church _____

Contact Name _____

Address _____

_____

Postcode _____

Telephone Number _____   Fax Number _____

E-mail _____

Fee for one-year licence: £11.75

These fees are valid until 31 December 2005. After that date please contact the Copyright Department for information.

Please enclose payment by cheque or fill in the details of your Visa/Mastercard number below.

| | | | | | | | | | | | | | | | | Expiry date until end _____

Signed _____

To be completed by Kevin Mayhew Ltd.

Payment of £11.75 received. Thank you.

Permission is granted subject to the following further conditions:

1. that the composer is acknowledged on every copy.

2. that the following copyright line is included on every copy:

    Copyright Kevin Mayhew Ltd. Reproduced by permission from *Music for Holy Week and Easter*.

    Licence Number _____   Licence expires on: _____

Signed for Kevin Mayhew Ltd. _____

Copyright Department, Kevin Mayhew Ltd, Buxhall, Stowmarket, Suffolk, IP14 3BW, UK
Telephone number: UK 01449 737978   International +44 1449 737978
Fax number: UK 01449 737834   International +44 1449 737834
E-mail: copyright@kevinmayhewltd.com   Website: www.kevinmayhewltd.com